Behold the Man

Behold the Man

A therapist's meditations on the Passion of Jesus Christ

BRIAN THORNE

Foreword by Robert Llewelyn

First published in 1991 by
Darton, Longman and Todd Ltd
1 Spencer Court
140–142 Wandsworth High Street
London
SW18 4JJ

This revised edition 2006

Reprinted 2008

ISBN-10: 0-232-52685-0
ISBN-13: 978-0-232-52685-1

A catalogue record for this book is available from the British Library.

Printed and bound in Great Britain by
Page Bros, Norwich, Norfolk

Contents

Foreword

This is not a comfortable book; one finds oneself too easily in its pages. But it is an encouraging and rewarding one for those who value self-knowledge and understand there can be no depth of spirituality without it.

These chapters found their beginnings in the traditional three hours devotional service of the Church of England. On learning of the impact the addresses made on the congregation I asked Brian Thorne if I might see his text and later pressed him to develop his theme and offer it to a wider public.

In his consideration of the interplay of personalities in the Passion narrative, which forms the body of the book, the author draws out how Jesus alone is free. Alone among the characters Jesus remains in touch with the centre of his being, thus remaining true to himself though completely stripped of human dignity. Herein lies the secret of his capacity to respond to hatred with full forgiveness, and to pour out his love in a measure we can scarcely begin to understand.

As a therapist the author tells his readers to understand the importance of discovering (as did Jesus) their true identity and to become aware of their infinite value in the sight of God. In this task there is often the need to separate false and morbid guilt (for which 'religion' is frequently responsible) from that which is healthy and appropriate, in the owning of which forgiveness may be found, opening the way to contact with one's true centre. Our goal is to accept our unique identity acknowledging that we are wholly acceptable and desirable to God. We are to come to love ourselves for the sake of God, which far from being selfish in the ordinary sense is (as it moves to perfection) a love purged of impurity of motive, and as a necessary corollary carries with it the love of all creatures for the sake of him who made them.

The author, who is trained in the influential school of Carl Rogers, is sought out daily by those from within and beyond the Church who are searching for inner healing. I believe many will be grateful for the spiritual insights in this book, combined, as they are, with the perceptions and skills of a trained psychotherapist.

ROBERT LLEWELYN

Preface

There are certain people without whose help and encouragement this little book would never have seen the light of day. I offer my thanks to them all for their loving support: to David Clark for inviting me in the first place to give these addresses; to Robert Llewelyn for insisting that they deserved a wider public; to Teresa de Bertodano and Esther de Waal for gentle encouragement along the way; to Christine Jope for uncomplaining and meticulous work on the word processor; and, as always, to my wife, Christine, for continuing to love a husband who spends half his life behind a closed door with other people.

BRIAN THORNE

Preface to the 2006 Edition

When this little book was first published in 1991, I little thought that sixteen years later it would be re-issued for a new readership. It would seem that although the book went out of print some years ago, it has continued to be valued by many individuals and also by some church congregations who have managed to collect battered early copies for corporate study during Lent or at other times. It is also heartening to know that an Indian edition appeared in 1997 and that a French translation, *Voici l'Homme*, became available in 1999.

In the intervening years my own life as a person-centred therapist and writer has been much enhanced by my encounters with increasing numbers of clients and trainees and with fellow practitioners in many parts of the world. Not infrequently these encounters have been characterised by the search for meaning in our increasingly desperate times and by a yearning for the restoration of trust in the capacity of humankind to find hope beyond despair.

It would seem that when *Behold the Man* first appeared it confronted many readers with the startling challenge of living the life of a new humanity. The passion and crucifixion of Jesus reveals to us our own inherent glory. If we truly believe that we are no longer servants but bound to Jesus in eternal friendship then we can perhaps perceive within ourselves something of our own divine inheritance.

In company with the great mystics of the Orthodox tradition we begin to glimpse the implications of perceiving Jesus as the prototype of what human beings have it within them to become. We are brought face-to-face with the challenge of theosis, that is, the insistent invitation to grow more and more into the likeness and image of God. The passion and crucifixion with their culmination in the resurrection assure us that theosis is not a destiny solely reserved for us in the life to come. It is possible for us in this life to participate in the divine energies which constitute the essential ground of our being, and so to enter into the eternal dance of love which is the life of the Holy Trinity.

As I reflect on the therapeutic journeys in which I have been privileged to participate over the years, I believe I have seen the marks of this movement towards the divine image in so many of my clients and trainees. Those who have arrived on the therapist's doorstep as fearful and self-rejecting individuals have frequently found within the challenging security of the therapeutic relationship the ability to accept that they are accepted. With this profound shift comes the liberating revelation that they have it within them to experience not only their own belovedness but also their capacity to be infinitely loving. For many the notion of being the friend of Jesus and the children of God assumes an altogether more powerful significance, and life is no longer a burden but the context for transformation where every day offers the prospect of a new way of being.

It is my hope that this new edition of *Behold the Man* will provide sustenance for those who in our own times dare to acknowledge what Mother Julian proclaimed over six hundred years ago when she stated that our souls are joined to God and always will be. Our willingness to accept and to live out this truth may well determine the future of the human race as well as the survival of the suffering planet on which we all depend.

I dedicate this edition to Father Robert Llewelyn who kindly provided the Foreword for the original publication, and who, as he approaches his ninety-seventh birthday, continues marvellously to inspire all those who yearn to find in Jesus, the incarnate Son of God, not only the glorious validation of their humanity but also the assurance of their divine calling.

BRIAN THORNE
Norwich 2006

Acknowledgements

Extracts are used by permission of the following publishers:

Cairns Publications: *Prayer at Night* by Jim Cotter, 1983; Collins: *Dance in the Dark* by Sydney Carter, 1980, and *The Dance of Love* by Stephen Verney, 1989; The Movement for the Ordination of Women and Women in Theology: *All Desires Known* by Janet Morley, 1987; Mowbray, a division of Cassell plc: *Unutterable Beauty* by C. A. Studdert Kennedy, 1983; Oxford and Cambridge University Presses: *New English Bible* second edition, 1970; Penguin Books Ltd: *Revelations of Divine Love* by Julian of Norwich, translated by Clifton Wolters, 1966; University of Wales Press: *Presenting Saunders Lewis*, edited by Alun R. Jones and Gwyn Thomas, 1973; WCC Publications, World Council of Churches, Geneva: *Weep Not For Me: Meditations on the Cross and the Resurrection* by John V. Taylor, 1986.

1

Introduction

When my friend, David Clark, Rector of Oadby, invited me to give the addresses at the traditional Good Friday services in his parish, I felt both privileged and apprehensive. I sensed that such an undertaking would involve confronting the central doctrines of the Christian faith and I knew, too, that I would be standing in a pulpit on the day in the Christian year perhaps most charged with emotion.

My decision to accept the invitation was prompted by a number of seemingly unrelated factors. In the first place, the beginnings of my own Christian commitment stem from a profound experience which occurred on Good Friday 1946 when I was a boy of nine. For me the encounter with the suffering Christ on that day gave meaning to my life. Secondly, as a therapist I spend much of my life being a companion to those who are in pain and I could dimly sense the challenge of what it might involve to attempt to enter empathically into the sufferings of Jesus at the time of his greatest torment and into the minds of those caught up with him in the events leading to Calvary. Thirdly, I had in the previous three months read four books all of which had made a profound impression on me and which tended to confirm many of my own discoveries along the path of Christian commitment. Gradually I began to realise that David Clark's invitation might enable me to articulate, within the rigorous framework of five brief addresses, at least some of my own deepest struggles as I attempt to be a Christian in the world of the late twentieth century. The books by Stephen Verney (*Water into Wine*), John Taylor

(*Weep Not For Me*) Donald Allchin (*Participation in God*) and Jim Cotter (*Prayer at Night*) were my constant sources of encouragement and stimulation.[1] More than that, the very knowledge that four such priests exist within the ranks of the Church of England assures me that, despite much recent evidence to the contrary, my own beloved part of the Anglican Communion can still offer the kind of acceptance, understanding and openness which my soul requires for its proper nourishment. I hope these gifted men will forgive my plunderings of their treasures.

The six meditations which follow (one has been added especially for this book) are based on the original addresses and are preceded by a brief autobiographical account of my experiences as a boy on Good Friday 1946. They are interspersed with quotations and prayers selected in the main by John Taylor and Jim Cotter and are each followed by questions to aid personal reflection or group discussion. They end with one of Charles Wesley's hymns which appears in Donald Allchin's masterly exploration[2] of the doctrine of theosis (divinisation by grace) as it is expressed by a number of representative Anglican figures in the past. My predominant reliance on St John's Gospel was almost inevitable after my reading of Stephen Verney's inspired introduction to its astonishing riches.

The book concludes with an extended discussion of the personality of Jesus as revealed in the Passion narrative and its relevance to the work of a therapist. The two appendices contain St John's account of the Passion and a guide to aid those who might wish to use the Passion narrative as

[1] Stephen Verney, *Water into Wine: An Introduction to John's Gospel* (London, Collins, Fount 1985); John V. Taylor, *Weep Not For Me: Meditations on the Cross and the Resurrection* (Geneva, World Council of Churches, 1986); A. M. Allchin, *Participation in God: A Forgotten Strand in the Anglican Tradition* (London, Darton, Longman and Todd, 1988); Jim Cotter ed, *Prayer at Night* (Cairns Publications, 1983).
[2] *Participation in God.*

a resource for personal meditation through the development of sustained empathy.

We are on this earth that we may learn to bear the beams of love . . .
(William Blake)

Autobiographical Prelude
The God Who Comes: Good Friday 1946

Good Friday 1946 found me playing cricket in a Bristol park which was still full of air-raid shelters and all the bric-a-brac of war. Suddenly there appeared in the street at the side of the park a procession of witness headed by a crucifer, candle bearers and a thurifer swinging a censer. The effect on me was instantaneous. I left my friends, ran all the way home and shut myself in my bedroom and sobbed for what seemed like hours. In the midst of this overwhelming distress I encountered the living Jesus and from that day until this I have had an unshakeable conviction that love is the primary force in the universe no matter how great the evidence may seem to the contrary. Looking back on it, the events of that Good Friday afternoon probably determined the direction of my life because they impinged on me at so many different levels. In the first place the initial incident was visually stupendous: the contrast between the solemn beauty of the procession and the barrenness of the park still ravaged by war could not have been greater. Secondly, the experience established in a moment an order of values. I suppose I felt mildly guilty that I was playing cricket on Good Friday but the main feeling was one of quite overwhelming gratitude that I could be so incredibly loved. In that moment I knew that in the last analysis all that matters is loving and being loved. I also knew that the love I had experienced brought with it a sense of being fully and profoundly understood.

It followed therefore that to love in this way must involve the deepest commitment to understanding. I have since discovered that love devoid of understanding, although it can bring comfort and solace, can never heal. Thirdly, the incident endowed me with an intoxicating sense of my own unique value. At a wholly conscious level I knew that something special had happened to me which I would never be able to deny or eradicate.

I suspect that my 'Good Friday' experience strikes chords for many people. One of the things we know from the recent research that has gone on into mystical experience is that thousands of us actually have such experiences (some have suggested as many as one in five) but that we seldom talk about them and often, indeed, dismiss them or succeed in banishing them from consciousness. I suppose it is not altogether surprising that we should behave in this way. At a time and in a culture where the so-called scientific method still rules the roost and objective knowledge is enthroned it is perhaps too much to expect that we should take such experiences with the utter seriousness which I am convinced they merit. They come as gifts but also as challenges to our concept of reality and it is sad in the extreme when as a result of conditioning we dismiss them as unimportant or even crazy.

I was very lucky (if luck can ever be the right word) to have my experience at the age of nine before those habits of thought had been formed which tend to dismiss subjective knowledge and experience as at best suspect and at worst a positive hindrance to the acquisition of the objective knowledge which alone is believed to have real value. Returning to my experience in the park there is one aspect of it which merits more detailed exploration.

Undoubtedly the most important and life-transforming outcome was the sense of being loved beyond all the possible limits of my imagining. I know and have known intermittently ever since that I am *desired* by someone or something who has created me and of whom I am in that

sense a part. There are, of course, many times – indeed so
many times that it becomes *most* of the time – that such a
notion seems patently absurd. In the first place I experience myself all too frequently as being pretty undesirable.
I have some abominable habits and I seem to have been
perpetrating the same sins for decades. Secondly, it seems
remarkably arrogant to claim that *I* am the desired of God,
that God finds *me* infinitely desirable. Yet I know that what
I experienced all those years ago is the essential truth about
me and what is more that if it is true of me it is true of all
of us. The corollary of all this is that self-hate, self-
contempt, self-denigration and all those other states of
mind which tell me that I am no good, that I am unworthy,
that I am worthless – all these gloomy self-judgements are
a denial of the truth about myself and separate me from a
compassionate and forgiving self-love which is the only
possible attitude towards myself in the light of the astound-
ing fact that God finds me desirable.

My experience was given to me on Good Friday. The
sobbing in my bedroom took place under a picture postcard
(very stylised) of the crucifixion on Calvary and I have
tried hard to reconstruct the words of Christ to the nine
year old me on that day. At the time, of course, the conversation was wordless – it was heart to heart. I can only
reconstruct it in the light of the message that still today
has not been fully revealed and perhaps never will be in
this world. Certainly I know what it was *not*. Jesus did *not*
say to me:

You know, you are a very naughty boy, more naughty
that you can ever know. In fact, if you knew the whole
story as I know it, you would realise that you actually
helped murder me. But you needn't worry. I care about
you so much that I actually chose to let you and all your
other friends in the human race murder me so that you
could experience how utterly forgiving I am and that I
can triumph over your evil. You see, you couldn't really

finish me off and however awful you are I really do love you and if you trust me and believe me you'll get a lot better and then you can really be my friend.

No, Jesus did not, I am convinced, talk to me like that. If he had I should have been terrified and I should have wondered how on earth I was ever going to be able to forgive myself enough to merit the friendship of such a superior and strange being. I reckon that what Jesus said was more like this.

Hello, Brian. It's lovely to have you near me. I'm so glad you're still alive after this dreadful war. I've tried to look after you and I hope you're not feeling guilty about playing cricket because it's a good game. Why I interrupted was to let you know something very important. You know already that life isn't always easy. People do terrible things like dropping bombs and it is very difficult to go on loving them. You get frightened, don't you, and upset and I bet you often feel you're not much good especially when people tell you off or get angry with you. Well, what I wanted to say was that you needn't be scared of people because they do awful things and you certainly need not be scared of dying. People did awful things to me and I died but I want you to know that it's all right. Whatever you do, don't let people tell you you're no good and go on trying to find out more and more what's going on. Most people don't want to know, it seems, but that's only because they're frightened.

I have come to believe that Jesus spoke to me somewhat like this in 1946 because such a message makes sense of much that has happened since. It explains why, over the years, sometimes, it seems, against all the odds, I have managed to keep a shaky hold on the truth that I and with me all humanity are infinitely desirable and why, too, I

8

have come to believe that self-awareness and self-knowledge must be pursued, however frightening, and however inimical they are to the part of us which wants a quiet life and resists growth and development. I was delighted to read recently in a book by the Catholic theologian, Sebastian Moore,[1] that he has come to believe that the original, generic sin is precisely this refusal to grow, this resistance to self-awareness. And, of course, such a resistance is closely linked to the feeling that I am no good. If I am no good I do not wish to discover more about myself. It is only when I feel good with conviction that I can go forward to discover more with confidence. Moore points out with telling force that we have now arrived at a situation where all the best counsellors and therapists are coming to understand the root of our evil as a bad self-image, a devaluing of self, while Christians tend to say in response, 'Ah, but you are forgetting original sin' – not realising apparently that the counsellors are precisely *pointing* to original sin – namely that attitude of mind which says, 'Human beings are hopelessly flawed and cannot therefore change'.

Questions for Reflection

1. What 'mystical' experiences have you had and how much attention have you paid to them?
2. How much is your love of God based on fear or guilt?
3. Do you agree that love devoid of understanding can never heal?
4. How does the doctrine of original sin affect your view of human nature?

[1] *Let This Mind Be In You* (London, Darton, Longman and Todd, 1985).

The pain of the world will not cease until its dark places have been penetrated with light, the light of understanding that uses the power of the dark to create . . . And that will not happen until we all come together to acknowledge the pain, to understand, to create . . .

(Jim Cotter, 'Prayer at Night')

3

Corporate Betrayal

It was night. (John 13:30)

As the climax of the Passion narrative approaches, the forces of darkness gather about Jesus with what seems like an inexorable momentum of their own. As Judas leaves the group and goes out into the night it seems that love is rendered powerless even at the most intimate level of friendship. It is, in fact, a terrible moment in the human drama. Judas has been in the company of Jesus for three years: he has experienced at close quarters the greatest love that the world has ever known and for much of that time we can only assume that he has responded to that love warmly and spontaneously. Certainly it would seem that he has worked hard for it is he who has been responsible for money management and for the distribution of alms. He was, one assumes, an intelligent man and the others must have held him in esteem. And now at this crucial time he goes out to hand over the Prince of Light to the Prince of Darkness. For some reason he can no longer respond to the love so freely offered and determines instead to work for its destruction.

In human relationships the story is only too common. Two people love each other and enter into a commitment. They promise to cherish and care for each other and to dedicate themselves to each other's wellbeing. And then after a while it all goes wrong. Boredom enters in, frustration, anger, jealousy or indifference. What began full of hope and the best of intentions ends in bitterness and separation. The same can happen between parents and children. Only a week or so ago I listened to the agony of a divorced mother whose only son had, without apparent reason, turned against her, left home and thrown up his place at college. For that woman it was night indeed. She cried out in her grief, 'I love him so much and now he seems determined to punish me beyond endurance.'

Let us try to face the darkness. It is only too easy to protect ourselves from it by seeking security in our bourgeois culture or even by coming together in a holy huddle in church. Good Friday is not the time for such evasion. There is something of brutal realism in Christ's words when he said to the daughters of Jerusalem, 'Do not weep for me: weep for yourselves and for your children.' He commands us not to seek refuge in false emotion but to look at ourselves and at the world and not to flinch from the evidence of what we see. Judas, when he left the Upper Room, was rejecting love: indeed he went out in order to set in train a course of events which would lead to love being crucified on a cross. What is it in us which today leads to the same rejection and the same kind of murder? There are, of course, a number of glib answers possible. For Christians the typical response is to talk about original sin. This slippery and misunderstood doctrine has led many to think of human nature as corrupt or at best inclined to evil so that almost every example of human iniquity can be explained by the facile comment, 'It's human nature'. It's human nature to tell lies, to fiddle the income tax, to deceive one's partner, to beat the children, to ignore the starving, to lust for possessions, to reject the mentally ill, to harass the homosexual: ultimately it is human nature, by this analysis, to betray God with a kiss and to connive at his death on a cross. Judas, after all, was only being human.

In this and the subsequent meditations I want to challenge this concept of humanity and I want to do so by attempting imaginatively to come alongside Our Lord in the final hours of his life. I want us to participate in the Passion and Crucifixion by sharing in the mind of Jesus as he experiences what it means to be a man confronting his death. After all Our Lord was only being human.

As Jesus sits at supper he is filled with unease: the very time when he is stretched to the utmost in the expression of his loving – the feet-washing, the symbolic enactment of self-giving in the blessing and sharing of the bread and the wine, the intimacy of the group of friends with the man he loved most resting against his breast – in the midst of all this Jesus is anxious. He senses betrayal. So great is his anxiety that he gives voice to it: 'Someone is going to hand me over; someone here: that will be terrible for me but for the person who does it it will be even more terrible'. The others are appalled and break into loud protestations. John is incited to ask Jesus to be more specific but Jesus cannot bring himself to name Judas. Instead, he indicates him indirectly. But if we are to believe the account in John's gospel John himself is left in no uncertainty; Jesus makes it clear to John that Judas is the person. Even if all the others remain confused John knows. My hunch is that Peter did, too, and some of the others sitting close to Jesus.

If we believe that Jesus knew all along what was going to happen and if we believe that Judas was a mere puppet having to take his allotted role because this was part of the great plan laid down in Scripture, then I fear there can be no hope for us. This would mean that we are programmed, controlled, without freedom to grow or develop. It would also mean that we are quite beyond each other's reach, unable to choose intimacy or separation, closeness or distance, love or indifference.

As we attempt to enter the mind of Jesus as he and his disciples go out into the night I would suggest that we might be surprised at the confusion there. Undoubtedly he is in anguish about Judas. How can it be that so good a friend has turned against him? He will be longing for a change of heart in Judas: he will be consumed with a sense

13

of the powerlessness of his own love to keep Judas in relationship with him. But as I try to enter the mind of Jesus I find myself stumbling upon another and unexpected feeling which is somehow more disturbing. It is a sense of bewildered sadness at the behaviour of the beloved John and then by extension of all the others in the group. John, at Peter's request, had extracted from Jesus the identity of the betrayer. He knew therefore something of the enormity of what was about to happen. He certainly knew that Judas was not hurrying away to pay the bills. He did nothing – and the others did nothing. Not a word to Judas, not even the most feeble attempt to stop him, nobody to pursue him into the night to discover the source of his pain and bitterness. So Jesus leaves the Upper Room and goes out into the night, his heart breaking for Judas and weighed down with sorrow at the apparent indifference of the others to Judas's plight. It was as if they had been paralysed by the apparent powerlessness of his own love: if Jesus could not keep Judas within their company what hope had they? For Jesus, I suggest, it must have felt very different. Why was it, he must have asked himself, that nobody, not even John whom he loved so dearly, had been able to say to Judas: 'We love you, you are one of us: where are you going? what are you intending to do?' Why was it that not one of them had seen that Jesus's impotent love needed the expression of theirs to regain its power? Why had they not been able to see that being truly human is impossible on your own?

Questions for Reflection

1. How do you explain why the love of Jesus was powerless to hold the heart of Judas?
2. 'It is only human to reject the mentally ill and to harass the homosexual.' Do you agree?

3. What are the implications of believing that Jesus knew all along what was going to happen to him?
4. Do you know and can you describe the sadness which comes when someone you love fails to offer love to someone else whom you also love?

Guilt and fear drive out the love we seek, allies of a cold moralism, rigid and solemn . . .

(*Jim Cotter, 'Prayer at Night'*)

4

Jesus and the Evil of Religion

'We have a law; and by that law he ought to die.' (*John 19:7*)

It is never easy for those of us who belong to a religious group – and especially perhaps for those of us who are members of a state church – to face the shocking truth that Jesus went to his death hated and condemned by the religious leaders of his day. What is more they planned and plotted and stirred up their followers in order to achieve his downfall. Theirs was a deliberate, premeditated and passionately implemented campaign of destruction. And they did it in the name of the God of Israel and in order to uphold the sacred Law. They saw themselves and were seen by others as virtuous men, upholders of the faith and the protectors of the holy tradition. To see them as political schemers, more interested in humiliating Pilate than in having Jesus put to death is, I believe, to evade the full impact of the appalling truth – that virtuous God-fearing men can become murderers precisely because of their virtue and their God-fearing disposition. Not, of course, that one should be surprised by this. After all the history of Christendom down to our own times is packed full of examples of the same grim phenomenon. Perhaps in our own day holy Christian men connive at character assassination rather than literal murder and we should be grateful for this marginal improvement. Certainly, however, they continue to use the holy Law as found in Scripture as the blunt instrument with which to assault their loving but

17

disturbing victims. 'We have a law and by our law he ought to be defrocked and hounded out of office.'

Jesus, we must remember, loved his people and was steeped in the traditions of his forefathers. By many he was himself perceived as a rabbi, a teacher of the Law. Throughout his life, as far as we know, he worshipped in the synagogue and preached there. When he was aged twelve he was to be found in the great Temple at Jerusalem among the priests and scholars debating with them and asking them questions. In the days before his arrest he was once more in the Temple addressing the crowds. We need to remember all this as we attempt to enter the mind of Jesus as he watches the crowd approaching him in the garden, Judas at the head with the lanterns illuminating their weapons. Here is his friend of yesterday leading a band of people many of whom Jesus must have known well from his many hours spent in the Temple. He must often have chatted with the Temple guards and the other Temple officials. Malchus, the unfortunate servant who was to lose an ear, albeit temporarily, was probably well known to him. This then was not a band of strangers: they were his co-religionists, some of whom he would have instantly recognised. John's account of the meeting in the garden is extraordinary on several counts but chiefly because it suggests that Jesus was by now calm within himself. The agitation in the Upper Room and the agony of the prayer to the Father are replaced by a loving sadness which is all-pervasive. We are told that the band of soldiers and officials is momentarily stopped in its tracks as Jesus appears to them: they fall to the ground as if blinded in some way by the force of his presence. Moments later Jesus comforts Malchus and heals his ear. He is, it seems in command of himself and radiates love and power. *But* – and it is an enormous but – this power which can heal and dazzle is in other ways without strength. Jesus does not or cannot resist arrest and the men who have come to seize him continue in their task despite the evidence which they have themselves witnessed of his radiance and healing power. Jesus, in short, endures once again the experience of the impotence of his own loving. He is self-possessed, full of light and compassion and yet faced with the implacable force of religious zeal and hatred he is powerless to resist. The precise moment of the encounter is worth reflecting on in detail.

> Jesus went out to them and asked, 'Who is it you want?' 'Jesus of Nazareth', they answered. Jesus said, 'I am he.' And there stood Judas the traitor with them. When he said, 'I am he', they stood back and fell to the ground. Again Jesus asked, 'Who is it you want?' 'Jesus of Nazareth', they answered. Then Jesus said, 'I have told you that I am he.'

These two bold utterances of Jesus '*I am he*' confirm the striking picture of a man who is completely at home in his own identity. He is being fully himself – loving, healing, inwardly strong and composed. And yet a few moments later he is in bonds and is led away, an apparently helpless prisoner. People who are so firmly at home in their own skin are always impressive. They stand out from the crowd because they are not dependent on others for their own sense of self-worth. They are free to think their own thoughts, own their own feelings and express what they experience without giving way to their own fear of psychological or physical attack. It is clear that Jesus is impressive in this way and it is for this reason that momentarily the soldiers and officials are literally bowled over by his presence. They cannot bear a person who is so fully and assuredly himself. A moment's thought reveals to us that it is *precisely* the individual who is secure in his own identity, the person who with confidence can say, 'I am', that many religions find so threatening. Indeed it seems to be the particular talent of certain religious people to ensure that individuals can never develop such a sense of strength in their own identity. The weapon they choose is that of condemnation which in turn induces a deep sense of guilt in the victim so that he goes through life a psychological cripple unable to affirm the beauty and wonder of his own nature.

I recall some eleven years ago at an international conference in Paris convening an impromptu seminar for those who wished to explore the relationship between psychological and spiritual development and how, within half an hour of the start, almost the whole group was in tears as one member after another talked about their experiences at the hands of the churches – both Catholic and Protestant. I still remember some of the stories now. There was the man brought up in a Catholic boarding school where the staff – mostly priests – inflicted a vicious round of humiliating punishments for the smallest misdemeanours and seemed to derive sadistic satisfaction from inflicting corporal punishment on lonely and frightened young adolescents. There was the women who had had her mouth washed out with soap by a nun for saying the equivalent of 'shit' and then been made to stand barefoot in the chapel for an hour without moving. There was the account of a Calvinist minister who had told a fifteen year old that she was possessed by the devil and should on no account enter a chapel building. The stories were not only of priests, nuns and ministers but also of parents whose religious beliefs and practices seemed to make it impossible for them to relate to their children without at the same time judging them, condemning them and making them feel so burdened with guilt that life was almost intolerable. For me that impromptu seminar was saved from turning into a complete nightmare by the contribution of a Swiss woman who told how as an adolescent she, too, had felt utterly guilty, unable to find any virtue in herself and totally despairing. In her distress she had rung the bell of a house of the Jesuit fathers and had collapsed sobbing into the arms of the priest who opened the door to her. Strangely enough he did not welcome her in but instead himself left the house and taking her arm walked for two hours with her in a nearby park. At the end of that time, she said, her despair had lifted and for the first time for years she felt that she had value. It was only some years later that she discovered that the priest who had walked in the park with her was Fr Pierre Teilhard de Chardin. It is perhaps not without its significance that de Chardin himself, brilliant scientist and mystic, was later to prove too tiresome for the Jesuit order and the Catholic Church and was severely censured. His mind and heart were too free to be shackled by the bonds of so-called orthodoxy. For the moment I need to pause and reflect with great sadness on those countless individuals over the years who have come to seek my help because they were so loaded with guilt that life had become well-nigh impossible. None of those people as I recall it had done anything particularly appalling – there were no murderers or rapists, arsonists or swindlers. They were afflicted by a guilt which was elusive but all-pervading, a sense of being in the wrong, of never being able to please those whose love they craved, of being eternally without value.

As Jesus stands before Annas – and again we should not assume that the two men were strangers to each other – we are told, for example, that one of the disciples at least was an acquaintance of Annas – he remains impervious to the condemnation and no sense of guilt assails him. On the contrary Jesus speaks firmly, almost provocatively. 'Why do you question me?', he asks. 'I taught openly in the Temple. If you want to know what I said, ask them who listened to me.' For this defiant remark he receives a blow in the face from one of the policemen guarding him and is accused of gross insolence. Again he does not flinch or capitulate. He does not accept the accusation and he refuses to feel guilty. Instead he replies, 'If I spoke amiss, state it in evidence against me: if I spoke well why do you hit me?'

Here then we see once more a man who is utterly secure in his own identity and who cannot be touched at the core of his being by the false accusations of the religious leaders. And, of course, they are infuriated. To their followers they portray Jesus as the blasphemer, the threat to national honour and to the faith of their forefathers. It is likely, too, that Annas, Caiaphas and the other chief priests genuinely saw it as their responsibility to preserve the Jewish nation and the Jewish faith. At a deeper level, however, we see the insidious workings of the lust for power and the egocentric craving to retain personal power and to preserve the absolute authority of the ecclesiastical institution. That is why religion can be a most destructive force in the life of human souls: it lends itself to an unscrupulous authoritarianism which cannot bear the uniqueness of persons and which beneath a cloak of virtue seeks to destroy those who by their inner security threaten its domination. As Jesus stands before Annas and then before Caiaphas he suffers the depth of anguish which comes from being truly himself only to discover that in doing so he is despised, condemned and rejected by those who profess to serve the same God that resides in his own heart. But Jesus does not succumb: he admits no guilt, he refuses to accept the judgement, his light reveals the darkness of his accusers. He is the great I am and his identity remains unshaken even in the midst of the most intense internal suffering. Not all can be so resolute: in another part of the courtyard, Peter is busily saying, 'I am not'.

Questions for Reflection

1. How comfortable do you feel with the attitudes and behaviour of leaders in your Church or with the views expressed by fellow Christians?
2. Do you agree that many religious people feel deeply

threatened by the person who is secure in his or her own identity?

3. Have you experienced primitive judgementalism from other Christians and, if so, how have you responded?

4. Why is it, do you suppose, that so many people seem to go through life weighed down by a great sense of guilt and unworthiness?

Lord, we remember all those who, because of their caste or class, colour or sex, are exploited and marginalised – the forces of oppression that trample on people and the unjust systems which break the spirit of people, and rob them of their rights and dignity.

Out of the depths we cry to you, Lord
Hear our cry and listen to our prayer.

Lord, we call to mind all authority that treats people as nobodies – military regimes and dictatorships, lonely prisons and unjust laws; the war industry and political greed.

Out of the depths we cry to you, Lord
Hear our cry and listen to our prayer.

> *(Intercession for Asia Sunday, 3 June 1984,*
> *quoted in John V. Taylor, 'Weep Not For Me')*

5

Jesus and Political Power

'You are not Caesar's friend.' *(John 19:12)*

Perhaps, like me, you have always had some sneaking sympathy for Pontius Pilate. I imagine him as a man who never fulfilled his ambitions as a Roman administrator. His appointment as Prefect of Judea in AD 26 was not exactly a plum job and one can only imagine that Pilate hoped it would be short-term and would lead to greater things. In fact he remained in office for ten years, the second longest holder of the prefectship. If we are to believe the historical writings of Philo Judaeus and Flavius Josephus it seems that Pilate was a blundering, insensitive and often brutal fellow who was keen to show his loyalty to the Emperor by some manifestation of devotion to the imperial service. It is recorded that on one occasion he allowed Roman troops to bring their military standards into Jerusalem with the busts of the Emperor which were, of course, considered idolatrous images by the Jews. What is more he did it in an underhand manner and had the troops bring in and set up the images by night. The Jews orchestrated a massive sit-down and lie-down protest demonstration and Pilate had to back down. On another occasion it seems the Jews sent letters of protest to Rome about Pilate's behaviour and the Emperor himself intervened to make Pilate remove golden shields with the Emperor's own name on them that he had placed in his residence in Jerusalem. In short then Pilate, it seems, had a knack of doing things guaranteed to infuriate the Jews and thus lead to civil disturbances which in turn would get him a black mark in the Emperor's book.

When the chief priests accused him of not being Caesar's friend they knew they were hitting at a particularly tender spot. It was, in fact, a scarcely veiled threat. They were as good as saying, 'If you don't put this man to death we shall be reporting you to Rome and we shall tell the Emperor that you took no action against someone who is not only a blasphemer in our eyes but a direct threat to the Emperor's own rule.' Poor Pilate, he so wanted the Emperor's approval and once again he was threatened with a situation which could lead to his censure and possible recall to Rome in disgrace.

It is in the light of all this that I continue to feel my sneaking sympathy for Pilate. After all, he did make some effort to avoid committing Jesus to death. There can be little doubt that he believed Jesus innocent and had no wish to see him crucified. One of the Gospels (Matthew) records that his wife, by tradition a lady called Procla, had a message sent to him while he was with Jesus imploring him to be careful because she had had a disturbing dream about Jesus that previous night. Such a message must have weighed on him profoundly and made him all the more concerned to spare Jesus if he could. Pilate wriggles and squirms in order not to become Jesus's executioner: he pleads Jesus's innocence before the crowd, he offers them Jesus as the traditional prisoner to be released at the Passover, he symbolically washes his hands to try to be rid of the responsibility. But then, in the dismal words of John, 'At last to satisfy them, he handed over Jesus to be crucified.'

As we attempt to enter the mind of Jesus as he stands before Pilate we are caught up in the history of nations. Jesus the Jew confronts the representative of the occupying forces. Pilate, the Roman patrician, faces a man brought to him as a criminal by the leaders of a subjugated people. It is a meeting between the man at the top of the political pyramid and a trouble-maker from the mob. And yet the remarkable fact is that Pilate has no power at all to disturb the inner equilibrium of Jesus. In fact it is Pilate who is forced by his role into complete inauthenticity. For Jesus there is once again the experience of calmness and apparent powerlessness. In the garden he has been faced by the forces of religious zeal and hatred – now he is faced by political power and the result is the same. Just as the band in the garden had recognised Jesus's radiance but had gone on to arrest him, so Pilate recognises Jesus's innocence but goes on to condemn him.

Jesus, it is clear, tries to communicate to Pilate. He tackles him on the source of the idea that he is a king but Pilate is merely angry and seems insulted as if he is being accused of being a Jew himself. His racial prejudice is such that he cannot engage with Jesus in rational discourse. The climax of their meeting is reached when Jesus states that his task is to bear witness to the truth and Pilate replies in the words which have made him infamous down the centuries: 'What is truth?' Jesus suffers the agony of sensing the man behind the politician and not being able to reach him. Pilate for his part is hopelessly caught. He recognises the innocence of Jesus but his fear and hatred of the Jews make it impossible for him to act on his perception. More than that he is also the prisoner of his own cynicism. His question, 'What is truth?', is the cynical comment of a man who has come to live a life ruled by political expediency and by the fear of forfeiting power. Truth is the last thing with which he can be concerned: he has instead to think of what will please the Emperor and preserve his own skin and position. The dialogue is an amazing one. It is not Jesus who is troubled in spirit. He speaks directly and unambiguously and is then flogged and repeatedly humiliated. But he retains his inner strength and is prepared to maintain silence as Pilate seeks to question him further. He even has the compassion to focus on Pilate's mounting guilt feelings and to speak words of comfort: 'The deeper

27

guilt lies with the man who handed me over to you.' No, it is not Jesus who is troubled but Pilate who is thrown more and more into confusion and agony of mind. No wonder, for he it is who becomes the channel for the corporate evil of the whole society gathered in Jerusalem at that time. There is no chance, it seems, for Pontius Pilate to be the person he had it in him to become: he has relinquished his personhood in the pursuit of power and wordly ambition so that faced by the pure humanity of Jesus he can recognise it but not protect it. This is a meeting between a fully-developed human being and a man who has squandered his humanity in the hunt for power. When Pilate eventually hands Jesus over he knows that he has lost the power struggle on all fronts. He has capitulated to the Jews and in the presence of The Man he has failed to be anything more than a pathetic provincial administrator who cannot even heed the promptings of his wife's unconscious.

How often does Jesus meet with Pilate in our day? In our own nation's life it would seem that it is becoming more and more difficult for politicians and administrators to avoid becoming, like Pilate, the channels for the corporate evil working in the institutions of the cosmos. Is the DSS official behind his plate glass window able to respond as a person to the distraught young mother whose cheque has not come through? Is the cabinet minister able to hear the cry of the prisoners whose major crime is to have fallen victim to the materialistic affluence which he has worked to create? As Our Lord spoke with Pilate in the year AD 33 he represented for all time the struggle of the individual human being to affirm the unique value of the person in the face of those who have surrendered their humanity to political ideology and the pursuit of power.

Pilate said to the Jews, 'Here is your King'. They shouted, 'Away with him! Away with him! Crucify him!' 'Crucify your King?' said Pilate. 'We have no king but

Caesar', the Jews replied. Then at last, to satisfy them, he handed Jesus over to be crucified.

Questions for Reflection

1. If Pilate recognised Jesus's innocence, why did he not release him?
2. Have you detected in yourself, or in others close to you, the loss of personhood which comes with the acquisition of power or influence?
3. Do you agree that we are now living in a society where it is more and more difficult for politicians to avoid becoming the channels for 'the corporate evil working in the institutions of the cosmos'?
4. How closely linked do you believe the abuse of power is to the kind of single-mindedness fired by political ideology?

Thus naked am I nailéd, O man, for thy sake!
I love thee, then love me; why sleepest thou? awake!
Remember my tender heart-rote for these brake,
With paines my veines constrainéd to crake.
                    (John Skelton, 'Woefully Arrayed')

6

Jesus and Those under Authority

That is what the soldiers did. (John 19:25)

Roman soldiers were disciplined men. Those who accompanied Jesus on the fateful walk to Golgotha had probably accompanied many convicted criminals before him. It was their job and it may seem unlikely that they would waste much thought or emotion wondering about the nature of the young rabbi whose inflammatory words and behaviour had earned him the death sentence. It was simply their task to carry out the most gruesome form of punishment known to the Roman Empire. Perhaps there was some sadistic pleasure in it but it is more likely that they felt demeaned by such sordid duties and longed for a more virile and admirable way of exercising their profession.

For Jesus himself the soldiers must have been a potent sign of the certainty of his destruction. They were themselves the powerless agents of superior authority and for them it would have been unthinkable to do anything other than carry out their orders. Not to have pushed him along the streets, not to have stripped him naked, not to have nailed him to the cross, not to have lifted that cross into its vertical position so that everyone could mock and gloat – not to have done any of these things would have been to fail in their duty and to court disgrace and probably their own execution. They were under orders and they had no option. In a sense, then, Jesus must have felt a strange sort of comradeship with his Roman captors for they were all

31

caught in the same apparent trap. But there was a crucial difference: he was accepting of his journey towards death whereas they had no option but to accompany him upon that journey.

Perhaps the role of a soldier engaged in internal security duties is about as gross an affront to personal authenticity as can be imagined. I recall my own experience as a national serviceman in Cyprus many years ago when as a young man I found myself caught up in the struggle of EOKA terrorists to shake off the domination of the British colonial authorities. During one particularly absurd week I found myself guard commander of a centre for women detainees who were suspected of being messengers or gun-runners for the terrorists. I was just twenty and my platoon were mostly teenagers from rural Gloucestershire: the detainees were almost all young Greek Cypriot women from high school. Emotionally the situation was an impossible one. In other circumstances the young men and women would have delighted in each others' company but in this grotesque situation the soldiers could have no contact with the women except that required by the ritual of the detention orders. One evening something inside me suddenly snapped. I suppose I could sense the onset of the internal desolation which always overwhelms me when I feel that I am about to lose hold of the core of my own identity. Whatever the reason I managed to engineer an hour when all the soldiers were occupied in various duties and I could talk furtively to the detainees not as the guard commander but as a person. They proved to me what I already knew. They were, in fact, the free ones and I was the prisoner. In their helplessness and vulnerability they were being true to themselves and their lives had meaning whereas I was the pawn of political and military forces which I could not control and which threatened to rob me of my identity. It is not for this realisation, however, that I chiefly recall that hour of intense and intimate conversation through the bars of police cell windows. It is rather for their loving response to me in that bizarre context that I shall always remember those young Greek Cypriot women. In their own powerlessness they were able to recognise that I was in the more appalling trap and they responded to my need. They gave me back a sense of my own dignity as a person and freed me from the shame of the role which I was compelled to enact.

I have no doubt that the loving understanding of unknown Greek Cypriot women towards a callow British second lieutenant is but a pale shadow of the feelings of the suffering Jesus towards the Roman soldiers who crucified him and tossed a coin for his tunic. Jesus throughout his life saw beyond the superficial appearances of those he encountered and he was always particularly drawn to those who seemed to have no power of their own. I am persuaded that in his heart he yearned to make contact with the persons hidden beneath the military uniforms and demeaned by the brutal behaviour which they were forced to inflict upon him. His surrendering of himself to them without resistance or struggle is a sign of his refusal to be anything but totally vulnerable and it is in vulnerability that love often makes itself most strikingly apparent. As he is nailed to the cross the heart of Jesus overflows in sorrowing love for those whose humanity has been so monstrously aggressed that they have no option but to carry out a legalised murder. This naked and utterly defenceless man cries out in agony not only because of intolerable physical pain but out of love for all those whose lives are in thrall to any authority which is blind to the wonder and fragility of human nature.

St John tells us that there were four soldiers whose duty it was to crucify Jesus and we can imagine that each had his particular responsibility. Perhaps one would have stripped Jesus while another held him down and the others hammered in the nails. It is, of course, an astonishingly intimate form of execution. Flesh touches flesh repeatedly and blood spurts everywhere. For Jesus there is the overwhelming proximity of the soldiers whose bodies were presumably young, athletic and full of animal vigour. In the normal course of events they might well have rejoiced in each other's energy and found pleasure in each other's company despite the difference of race and culture. As it is the initiative lies with the man who is psychologically free. We can never know how Jesus communicated his love and understanding to the soldiers who carried out his death sentence but it would seem that he can have done so only through the expressiveness of his tortured body. Flesh and blood are themselves the channels of love which communicate through the eyes of a dying man as he looks upon those under a dark authority and gives them back their humanity. A few hours later the centurion in charge of the crucifixion will bear witness to the fact that the love of Jesus has indeed broken through and irradiated the horrific climax of a sequence of events brought about by blind and corrupt power. 'Truly this was a son of God', he shouts and his words attest to the fact that love has penetrated the role of the man under orders and reached to the heart of a person who longs to be as free as the victim whose cruel death he has dutifully supervised.

> O saving victim, opening wide
> The gates of heaven to man below
> Our foes press on from every side
> Thine aid supply, thy strength bestow.

Questions for Reflection

1. Have you ever found yourself trapped in a role or function and been unable to salvage your humanity?
2. Imagine that you have lost your occupational role and your family relationships. Who are you now?
3. How is it possible to make contact with someone who hides behind a role?

4. Do you ever keep others out by maintaining a fixed role or adopting stereotyped attitudes and responses?

Jesus,
I imagine
how you must have loved Mary Magdalene
who was beautiful
and smelled of flowers.
When you put your arms round her,
her surrender
was as great
as a divine love.
                    (Ernst Eggimann, 'Jesustexte')

Christ, whose bitter agony
was watched from afar by women,
enable us to follow the example
of their persistent love;
that, being steadfast in the face of horror,
we may also know the place of resurrection,
in your name, Amen.
                    (Janet Morley, 'All Desires Known')

7

Jesus and Women

Near the cross where Jesus hung stood his mother, with her sister, Mary, wife of Clopas, and Mary of Magdala.

(John 19:25)

In my previous meditations I have tried to look at the power of religion and the power of political forces in order to understand their immense contribution to the crucifixion of Jesus. In some ways such reflections can keep us safely caught up in our intellects. They sanitise horror and make of it a subject for debate. It is like discussing the theology of apartheid rather than sharing imaginatively in the daily sufferings of an oppressed and humiliated people. But now the time has come to speak plainly of the brutality, hostility and hate in the Passion story. As John Taylor has shown so vividly, there is an unspeakable build-up of aggression and abuse as one group after another pile their hatred onto the defenceless body of this good man. It all seems so inexplicable. Why should so much violence have been discharged upon *this* man of all men? Why Judas's villainy, the man trusted with the common purse? Why should the teachers of the moral law, the Pharisees with their tremendous zeal for spiritual revival, be so set on getting rid of the young rabbi? Why were the high priests so utterly determined to drive the luckless Pilate to impose the sentence of death? Why did the guards in Caiaphas's hall suddenly start beating their prisoner about the head? Why did the normally well-disciplined Roman soldiers turn against their semiconscious victim with another vicious

37

burst of bullying? John Taylor suggests that if we are honest these questions are as unanswerable now as they were then. Somewhere in the world right now it is almost certain that an innocent victim is being viciously savaged by guards, police or interrogators. What is more, it is the innocent person who remains in control of himself who provokes the greatest rage in his oppressors. It is as if the torturers dimly realise that *they* are the ones without strength and the realisation is intolerable. The greater the light, it seems, the greater the darkness. The more calm and centred the innocence, the more the extreme brutality. It is as if total goodness is an affront which must be destroyed.

The Christ who hung on the cross, then, had been brutalised to a horrible degree. He was not even capable of carrying the cross-beam of his tree of execution and the passing Simon is coerced into service on the way to Calvary.

Mother Julian of Norwich does not shrink from telling us of the vision she had of the dying Jesus on the cross. The figure she sees is very far removed from the stylised image familiar to us from many a crucifix with its seemly loincloth and neatly contained wounds. This medieval mystic, much beloved in the city where I live, faced the full horror of the long drawn-out dying of a naked man who had been most viciously abused before he was even nailed to the cross.

That blessed flesh and frame was drained of all blood and moisture. Because of the pull of the nails and the weight of that blessed body it was a long time suffering. For I could see that the great, hard, hurtful nails in those dear and tender hands and feet caused the wounds to gape wide and the body to sag forward under its own weight, and because of the time it hung there. His head was scarred and torn, and the crown was sticking to it, congealed with blood; his dear hair and his withered flesh was entangled with the thorns, and they with it. At first, when the flesh was still fresh and bleeding the constant pressure of the thorns made the wounds even deeper. Furthermore, I could see that the dear skin and tender flesh, the hair and the blood, were hanging loose from the bone, gouged by the thorns in many places. It seemed about to drop off, heavy and loose, still holding its natural moisture, sagging like a cloth. The sight caused me dreadful and great grief; I would have died rather than see it fall off. What the cause of it was I could not see, but I assumed that it was due to the sharp thorns, and the rough and cruel way the garland was pressed home heartlessly and pitilessly.[1]

In this way a medieval woman beheld her Lord as he hung dying on the first Good Friday. So it was, we may imagine, that on that day the four women closest to the cross beheld the suffering Jesus. Three were members of his family including his mother, Mary, the fourth is the woman we know as Mary Magdalen – healed of mental illness by Jesus and certainly one who loved him profoundly and who was later to be the privileged person who first encountered the Risen Lord. These women display great courage in showing their love to the dying man despite the mockery and jeers of the crowd and they show what seems to be an absolute fearlessness in the presence of the deepest suffering. Among the men only John, it seems, shows equal courage and fearlessness.

The life of Jesus is rich with stories of his encounters with women and it seems somehow appropriate that he should die supported by the loving presence of women after most of the men had turned tail and fled. As we remember his moving and intimate conversations with his mother, with Mary and Martha from Bethany, with the Samaritan

---

[1] Julian of Norwich, *Revelations of Divine Love*, trans. Clifton Wolters (London, Penguin, 1966), pp.88–9.

woman at the well, with the woman with an issue of blood, with Jairus's daughter, with the widow of Nain, with the woman caught in adultery, it comes as no surprise to learn that Jesus was much loved by women. On the way to Golgotha we are told by Luke that great numbers of people followed, many women among them who mourned and lamented over him. Against the stark brutality inflicted by the religious, political and military *men*, the women symbolise the beginnings of compassion and understanding. Procla's dream-life reveals Jesus's innocence and the women of Jerusalem weep for the man they pity. On the way to the cross there is the beautiful tradition of Veronica who hands Jesus a napkin to wipe his bleeding face which is then forever imprinted on the fabric. At the foot of the cross the four women wait in sorrow and love.

It is strange how often the role of women in the final hours of Jesus's life is either overlooked entirely or given scant attention. It is as if the many male commentators on the Passion and Crucifixion are somehow loath to acknowledge that without the women there would be scarcely a redeeming feature in the whole grim story of brutality, viciousness and hate. What, one wonders, would have been in the mind of Jesus as he experienced this female presence during his hours of greatest anguish?

I can only imagine that he must have experienced a profound sense of being loved in the midst of the most unspeakable agony. He is utterly powerless, stripped, grievously wounded, a terrible sight to behold. And yet the women are there – as Julian many hundreds of years later was to be there in her vision – fully conscious of the horror and the overwhelming pain but full of love for the man who had changed their lives. It is indeed remarkable that for so much of its history the Church has been dominated by a concept of woman as Eve, the temptress – somehow unreliable and dangerous in her loving. But in his last hours Jesus is loved and supported by women whose love is faithful and fearless to the end. Jesus on the cross experiences the love of women as capable of taking on the cosmic forces of darkness. Here are the lovers who are truly fitting companions for love incarnate in the hour of his deepest torment and despair. The daughters of Eve become the lovers of Christ and the crucified Lord knows their presence as the hour of death approaches. Who is this nailed on a cross who seems to have earned the hate and hostility of the patriarchal world of religion and politics but for whom women weep in distress and love? Who is this man who loved the adulteress and the prostitute? Who is this God from whom men flee and to whom women give their love without fear?

Questions for Reflection

1. What do you find yourself experiencing as you share Mother Julian's vision of the dying Jesus on the cross?
2. In your own life do you experience women as more emotionally sensitive and resilient than men?
3. Why is it, do you think, that Jesus was so much loved by women?
4. Do you believe that in the history of the Church women have been denigrated by being categorised as the daughters of Eve?

God be in my head and in my understanding
God be in my eyes and in my looking
God be in my mouth and in my speaking
God be in my tongue and in my speaking
God be in my lips and in my greeting

God be in my nose and in my smelling/inhaling
God be in my ears and in my hearing
God be in my neck and in my humbling
God be in my shoulders and in my bearing
God be in my back and in my standing

God be in my arms and in my reaching/receiving
God be in my hands and in my working
God be in my legs and in my walking
God be in my feet and in my grounding
God be in my joints and in my relating

God be in my guts and in my feeling
God be in my bowels and in my forgiving
God be in my loins and in my swiving
God be in my lungs and in my breathing
God be in my heart and in my loving

God be in my skin and in my touching
God be in my flesh and in my paining/pining
God be in my blood and in my living
God be in my bones and in my dying
God be at my end and at my receiving.
                    (Jim Cotter, 'Prayer at Night',
                    after the Sarum Missal)

8

The Divinisation of Humanity

'It is accomplished!'. (John 19:30)

As the death of Jesus draws nearer minute by minute so
our task of trying to enter his mind and spirit becomes
increasingly difficult. We last thought of him caught in the
gaze of women who love him. We have shared his pain and
bewilderment at the treachery of Judas and the apparent
paralysis of the other men who had been his intimates for
three years. We have entered his inner calm and witnessed
his self-control as he is confronted by the frustrated fury of
religious and political leaders. We have perhaps dared to
imagine something of the unbearable physical pain and
anguish as he has endured the appalling assaults, beatings
and the final brutality of the most obscene and humiliating
punishment known to the Roman Empire.

Now, however, we are challenged at the deepest level by
the mysteriousness of his extraordinary personality. His
recorded words from the Cross weave a bewildering pattern
of despair and inner strength, of physical agony and astonishing detachment. As they are reported in the Gospels,
we hear:

Father, forgive them, for they do not know what they
are doing.

Eli, Eli lama sabachthani: My God, my God, why hast
thou forsaken me?

I tell you this: today you shall be with me in Paradise.

Mother, there is your son.

43

Son, there is your mother.

I thirst.

Father into thy hands I commit my spirit.

It is accomplished.

What are we to make of these utterances from the lips of a dying man? I would suggest that we can discover in them the agony and the ecstacy of what it means to be fully human. Here we see before our eyes and hear ringing in our ears what it truly means to be a human being. In the first place, Jesus is open to the full range of existential torment. He knows what it means to feel utterly desperate, abandoned by the God in whom he had placed his complete trust. He knows what it means to grasp the hope which lies beyond despair and to trust again against all reason. Secondly, he knows what it is to be open to relationship at every level. He receives the love and respect of the condemned thief and responds in fullest measure without the least trace of judgement or withholding. He is loved and hated with intensity. To the hatred he responds with complete forgiveness: to the love he responds with an outpouring of his own love which it seems we cannot even begin to understand. But to understand is our task if we are to enter into the mind and heart of Jesus. Let us then try once more to be with the dying Lord.

He sees through the blood and sweat of his agony and in the semiconsciousness of his dying hours, his mother – a middle-aged peasant woman who loves him passionately but who has let him go – and his dearest friend, probably a young man from a different class and of superior intellect. Both, he knows, will experience his death as the most appalling tragedy and their lives will be shattered. Jesus loves them with an intensity which transcends his agony. He joins them together, these two so different people, and we are told 'from that moment the disciple took her into his home'. Of course, this may simply mean that John gave

Mary a place to live in and some security in her desolation but I am persuaded with Stephen Verney that it means very much more than this. Jesus is asking his mother and his dearest friend to enter into each other's hearts, to establish the deepest bonds of intimacy. He is asking them to overcome differences of age and sex, of background and intellect and to be for each other as he has been for them. In short, he is inviting them to enter into a new reality of love which heralds a new age. This is what Jesus thirsts for and he thirsts for it in his physical anguish, in the body which is now dried up and parched, and in his spirit which yearns that we may find unity in our uniqueness and diversity.

When that final word comes from his lips, 'It is accomplished', we hear the proclamation that a human person has achieved the fullness of being. This is what is possible when a human being dares to be fully himself.

How supremely difficult it is for us to identify with the dying Jesus. To enter his mind and heart is to move into a world of mystery and paradox – of despair and hope, of naked and suffering flesh and of agonising yet finally triumphant spirit, of the intensity of love both received and given. Perhaps in some ways it is easier to be with the beloved disciple, John. He, remember, only a few hours previously had been powerless to stretch out to the treacherous Judas, but now he is at the foot of the cross, the only man who dares to give expression to his love and tenderness. What is more he responds to the request of the dying Jesus to find room in his heart for Mary and in so doing he demonstrates the kind of loving which he has himself received from his dying friend. Age, sex, background, intellect are no barrier: they melt away as love flows from the dying Jesus in the way that soon blood and water will flow from his dead and mutilated body.

Perhaps it is easier to identify with John because John is, as it were, one of us – a real human being not a mysterious Christ. In the same way we can perhaps dimly imagine the experience of Mary Magdalen on the first Easter morning as she blinks through her tears and sees the gardener. She, too, seems reassuringly human. But I am going to insist: our task is to dare to be with Jesus.

Let us go back to an earlier time when he was in danger of being stoned by the Jews. Listen.

> Once again the Jews picked up stones to stone him. At this Jesus said to them, 'I have set before you many good deeds, done by my Father's power; for which of these would you stone me?' The Jews replied, 'We are not going to stone you for any good deed, but for your blasphemy. You, a mere man, claim to be a god.' Jesus answered, 'Is it not written in your Law, "I said: You are gods"? Those are called gods to whom the word of God was delivered ... Then why do you charge me with blasphemy because I, consecrated and sent into the world by the Father said, "I am God's son"?'[1]

Here, then, is the awesome key which can begin to set us free to come alongside the dying Lord. The truth is that we find it so difficult to identify with Jesus because we are not reconciled to the mysteriousness of our own natures. We will not or cannot, it seems, accept what the Psalmist says in the very passage which Jesus uses to defend himself from the charge of blasphemy: 'We are gods yet we shall die like men.' We flee from the awesome, unbelievable truth that to be fully human is to share in the divine nature and that is why we want to distance ourselves from the dying Christ as if he is not really one of us at all. But he is *and* he is the Son of God as we are children of God. As our beloved friend he dies to show us what it means to accept our true natures. The cry 'It is accomplished' is the proclamation of the New Age which dawned on the first Good Friday. It tells us that God became man so that man

[1] John 10:31–42.

might become God. These are the words of Athanasius so brilliantly illuminated by Donald Allchin in his recent book *Participation in God*. As our dear Lord dies on the cross, if we are truly prepared to be with him we have no option but to recognise ourselves for the first time and to grasp what it means to be truly human. We are called to participate in the divine nature and to be taken into a relationship of complete intimacy with God. But Jesus could not do it on his own and nor can we. He needed the love of his Father but when he could no longer feel that love he rested in the love of women and the love of a man who had overcome fear and was free from the bonds of religious bigotry and political power games. In the end, it is not the mysteriousness of Jesus which is the stumbling block. It is the blinding clarity with which his death demonstrates to us the divine quality of our own natures and the fearlessness of the loving we need from each other if we are to be fully human. 'Behold the man', said Pilate – and in that statement he gave the answer to his own cynical question, 'What is truth?' The truth is within each one of us and what happened on Calvary challenges us to see it and not to be afraid. With such a vision and with such fearlessness we shall recognise that we are members one of another and we shall live in a new created world.

Questions for Reflection

1. What do you imagine were Jesus's feelings for his mother and for John as he hung on the cross?
2. Many people today talk of the New Age? Does this expression have any meaning for you?
3. At the end of his earthly life Jesus was abandoned by his Father but upheld by the love of a few friends, mostly women. Do you agree?
4. What would it mean for you to believe with Athanasius that God became man so that man might become God?

Let earth and heaven combine,
　　Angels and men agree,
To praise in songs divine,
　　The incarnate Deity,
Our God contracted to a span,
Incomprehensibly made man.

He laid his glory by,
　　He wrapped him in our clay;
Unmarked by human eye,
　　The latent Godhead lay;
Infant of days he here became,
And bore the mild Immanuel's name.

Unsearchable the love
　　That hath the Saviour brought;
The grace is far above
　　Or man or angel's thought:
Suffice for us that God, we know,
Our God, is manifest below.

He deigns in flesh to appear,
　　Widest extremes to join;
To bring our vileness near,
　　And make us all divine:
And we the life of God shall know,
For God is manifest below.

Made perfect first in love,
　　And sanctified by grace,
We shall from earth remove,
　　And see his glorious face:
Then shall his love be fully showed,
And man shall then be lost in God.
　　　　　　　　　(Charles Wesley)

9

A Therapist's View of the Passion Narrative

The Jesus whom we have accompanied through the appalling sufferings of the Passion narrative is at all times firmly in touch with the centre of his own being. If it were not so he would rapidly have been overwhelmed by events and would have ended as no more than a pathetic and misunderstood prophet executed by the Romans because they had been persuaded that he was a political threat: Jesus however is not overwhelmed. It is true that he is rendered completely powerless and stripped of every vestige of human dignity, but in the deepest recesses of his being he remains firmly in touch with his own authority. Even on the cross he is able to call up reserves of love and compassion which enable him to respond to his mother and friend and even, I have suggested, to those responsible for carrying out his execution. In short, he remains true to himself in the midst of the most savage assaults on his identity.

The preceding paragraph is, of course, a therapist's psychological interpretation of events. A biblical scholar might express things differently. He might point to the relationship which Jesus has with his Father and see him as delivering himself up into the hands of the Father, a process which only momentarily founders when he cries out in dereliction from the cross and seems to experience utter abandonment. On this understanding of events Jesus is sustained through his suffering not by his ability to stay in touch with himself but by his utter dependence on the will and support of God, the Father.

It can be argued, and indeed has been, that the two interpretations amount to the same thing. Christopher Bryant, for example, writing of St Augustine's famous dictum, 'O God, thou has made us for thyself and our hearts are restless until they rest in thee', has this to say:

> But if we understand the desire for God as the desire to be at one with our true centre, the desire to live in accordance with the truth of our being, then this ancient doctrine is infused with new and exciting meaning. The desire to rest in God will be seen as a desire to live from our centre to express our own truth, to be centred, integrated, a city at unity in itself.[1]

Bryant is here pointing to the concept of God within, a loving presence residing in the very heart of the individual which becomes indistinguishable from the person's deepest sense of identity. Creator and creature become united in the same substance.

For the therapist it is a daily experience to meet people who have no sense of their own identity and who endure life as fragmented beings with no awareness of the glory of being human. On the contrary they are customarily without worth in their own eyes and feel themselves to be unlovable. Not infrequently they are weighed down with shame at their own inability to relate to others and their total lack of trust that others will treat them with respect. It is the therapist's task – often conducted over many years and with many false starts and cul-de-sacs – to bring such people to an awareness of their own identity and to a trust in their essential value and goodness. The obstacles in the way of such a pilgrimage (for it is a spiritual journey) are formidable and in the Passion narrative they are illuminated with a chilling starkness.

[1] Christopher Bryant, *The River Within* (London, Darton, Longman and Todd, 1978), p.17.

The betrayal of Judas points to the fickleness of friendship and to the inability of even a close-knit group to respond to its individual members with love and understanding. And yet no human being can be human on his own and when Judas is left alone in his treachery there is nothing that can impede his descent into darkness. The disciples as they sat at supper on the first Maundy Thursday resemble many a family or friendship group where patterns of relationship contrive to produce a scapegoat usually through jealousy, envy or resentment. Judas, it seems, is made the receptacle for all the negative feelings in the group (for which of the disciples could have been totally free of anger against Jesus for having brought them into such danger and confusion?). It is Judas, therefore, who becomes the betrayer and sets out to destroy the love from which he now feels alienated.

Jesus himself emerges from the Upper Room deeply wounded by Judas and accompanied by those who will soon forsake him in the same way that they have abandoned Judas to his fate. Whereas Judas will later kill himself, however, Jesus will not fall victim to self-rejection. He will survive the emotional bludgeoning because he is at one with himself, or, as he himself is recorded as saying, 'The Father and I are one'. The intimate group destroys Judas but even when it does its worst it cannot undermine the trust of Jesus in his own identity.

Families and intimate groups nourish and sustain their members but they can also inflict the most exquisite pain usually through the withholding of love or through the creation of conditions for acceptance and approval. As a therapist I am regularly confronted by those who have suffered in this way and as a result are unable to experience their own value or to find meaning in the world. The state of self-rejection is alienation from the core of one's own being or, to use the other interpretation, it is separation from God who resides within. For me, therefore, the person who is caught up in self-rejection is experiencing hell.

51

When Judas leaves the Upper Room he is in hell and he remains there until the end of his earthly life. It is a grim thought that he may have been driven there by a lack of love and understanding on the part of the other disciples and that the love of Jesus for him was ultimately powerless in the face of the indifference or even hostility of the others. I am reminded of clients who are clearly loved by perhaps mother or father but who can no longer perceive or experience that love and know only the jealousy, contempt or hate of their siblings.

When Jesus appears before the High Priest he is face to face with those who will use all the weight of their authority and the religious tradition which they represent in order to destroy him. They succeed in their intention insofar as they bring about his crucifixion but at another level they fail completely. They are totally unable to induce in Jesus those feelings of overpowering guilt which destroy the personality and leave an individual without hope of forgiveness. The purveyors of such annihilating guilt are often to be found in the ranks of the religious and again as a therapist I am all too familiar with their victims. Their viciousness resides in their ability to create a total view of reality (religions are customarily expected to explain everything) so that those in whom guilt has been induced have no way out of their predicament except abject capitulation. The therapist working with such a client has the painful and painstaking task of enabling the guilt-sufferer to dismantle brick by brick the edifice of the religious prison in which he or she is incarcerated. The work is rendered the more complex by the need to separate out the annihilating and inappropriate guilt induced by the religion-mongers from the healthy and appropriate guilt which unerringly points to those obstacles which are preventing individuals from making contact with the core of their own being. The God of this kind of religion, it seems, seldom bears much resemblance to the God whose presence is to be found within.

Jesus in his confrontation with Pilate encounters the embodiment of corrupt secular power and refuses to be intimidated. In the same way that he rejects the guilt-inducing power of the religious authorities, so, too, he refuses to enter into dialogue with Pilate. In some ways this demands even greater self-assurance for Pilate certainly believed that he had authority to release Jesus and, given reassuring noises, would undoubtedly have tried to do so. Colluding with those in power is a sure way of losing personal integrity and yet the process is often subtle and seductive. The lust for power lurks in the hearts and minds of even the most unlikely people and again the therapist meets with monotonous regularity those who have betrayed themselves for a whiff of power and prestige and no longer know how to retain their own identity. Such a fate often befalls those who are particularly gifted and have great talents to exercise for the good of the community. The sad tales of their often spectacular downfalls do much to help fill the columns of the gutter press. When Pilate is told that his power is worthless and that he has no real authority he hears what many discover through the personal tragedy of gaining an ephemeral power at the cost of their own souls.

The soldiers who carry out the act of crucifixion are trapped in a role from which there is no escape. I have suggested that Jesus himself was able to see beyond the role and to make contact with the people behind the military uniform; we might even take comfort from imagining that after the horrific events on Calvary the soldiers found a way of discovering personal liberty. Their predicament, however, illuminates the insidious way in which the roles that we assume can obscure us from others and even ourselves. We can become so caught up in playing the part of our occupation or professional persona that we lose our anchorage and turn into a caricature of a person, divorced from our centre. The role takes on its own authority, whether or not we are literally under the authority of others, and in its name we fall into the habit of performing actions and even thinking thoughts which are nothing less than a succession of self-betrayals. In the last month I have shared the desperation of a man, distinguished and respected in his profession, who has made the shattering discovery that he is on the very edge of ultimate self-betrayal. He knows that he must resign his position and perhaps even leave his marriage for there, too, he realises that he is no more than an actor, a shell of a person who no longer knows where to locate the source of his being.

As we have followed Jesus through the stages of his Passion we have encountered a man able to withstand the rejection of his intimates, to refute the accusations of the religious authorities without succumbing to guilt, to turn his back on the seductive invitation to collude with corrupt power and to avoid the trap of confusing either himself or others with the roles that are enacted. In short, we discover a person who avoids with triumphant assurance the pitfalls into which so many clients coming for therapy have plunged headlong. Here is a man, in Christopher Bryant's words, who is clearly 'at one with his true centre and living in accordance with the truth of his own being'. It remains now to throw more light on why this is so and clearly it is not good enough simply to affirm that Jesus is the Son of God and would therefore by definition not require psychotherapy! If, as I have argued, we are all sons and daughters of God, it may not be without value to attempt a more penetrating study of our brother, Jesus, so that we may more readily perceive the way to human fulfilment and hence to the divinisation of the human family.

Questions for Reflection

1. Do you agree with Fr Christopher Bryant that the desire for God and the desire to be at one with our true centre are the same thing?

2. Have you ever been made the scapegoat in your own family or circle of acquaintances or have you joined in scapegoating someone else?
3. Do you believe that religious belief should provide a total and detailed view of reality?
4. How much does the love of power operate in your own life and what are the effects of this in your personal and professional life?
5. What steps would you need to take if you were really concerned to be at one with your own true centre and to live in accordance with the truth of your own being?

10

The Personality of Jesus
and the Process of Therapy

It is clear from the Gospel narratives that Jesus was a special person from the very moment of conception. Whatever we may or may not believe about angels, virgin births or the operation of the Holy Spirit, there can be no doubt that Mary and Joseph knew that their child was special. The place and manner of his birth may have been humble in the extreme but his welcome into the world was exceptional. The stories of adoring shepherds, rejoicing angels and worshipping Magi simply serve to reinforce the sense of wonder and celebration at the arrival of a precious and uniquely special human being into the world.

This, then, is what human beings deserve as they make their way into life but in our Western culture only a tiny number are lucky enough to experience even a pale reflection of such a welcome. The fortunate few have a mother who rejoices at their presence in her womb and is filled with a sense of joyful wonder at their coming into being. They have a father who surrounds the mother with loving protection and is prepared to take bold decisions when he senses that danger lurks for the unborn child. They are received into a wider community where their birth is a signal for celebration and delight. More commonly, however, the passage into life for the newborn is very different. Mothers are often anxious about or even hostile towards what is growing in their bodies. Fathers frequently have scant understanding of a woman's experience and afford little support or protection during the mother's months of pregnancy. In many cases today the wider community has no interest in the birth and even family bonds are often so tenuous in a highly mobile society that there can be no assurance of family involvement and support. The welcome into the world, in short, can be uncertain and in many instances there is only coldness or indifference. For some children their experience, far from being akin to that of Jesus, is more reminiscent of that of the Holy Innocents. Metaphorically they are murdered before they are two years old.

The sense of Jesus's specialness is still very much in evidence as he approaches adolescence. The story of the visit to the Temple in Jerusalem shows us a boy who is confident enough in himself to keep company with the scholars of the day and not be overawed by their authority. What is more, Mary and Joseph are able to overcome their own pain and anxiety at their son's apparent precociousness and lack of concern for their feelings; his mother is able to ponder these things in her heart and to be at peace with herself. This incident provides a remarkable insight into the family home in which Jesus grew up. Clearly he is not only deeply loved but also respected so that he is able to exercise the freedom to display his own remarkable gifts without fear of being adversely judged or rejected. One outcome of this, it seems, is that he does not find it difficult in turn to respect his parents and to be subject to their authority in most aspects of his daily existence.

The willingness to conform is at first sight surprising in one who is to become the most radical nonconformist in human history. Yet there seems little doubt that Jesus for the most part grew up in conformity with the conventions and practices of his day. He learned a trade (lovingly instructed perhaps by Joseph), worked as an ordinary member of society, attended the synagogue and was steeped in the tradition of his culture. It would seem, however, that this apparently conventional existence was serving all the while to nourish his inner sense of identity and to strengthen the deep sense of his unique vocation.

The concept of vocation often receives a poor press these days and yet it is evident that from a very early age Jesus was a person with a vision of his own meaning and purpose. This is not to suggest that he knew what it was he had to do in any precise terms and yet it is clear that his 'Father's business' was what informed his deepest longings. I am tempted to believe that persons who have been truly welcomed into the world and whose specialness is beyond any doubt in the eyes of those who love them have every chance of discovering a meaning and purpose. They become literally 'visionaries' in the sense of being drawn slowly and irresistibly towards the illumination of their own destiny.

It could be argued that at the age of thirty Jesus was ready to fulfil the meaning of his life because up to that point he had experienced a totally exceptional validation of his being in the world. Treasured and respected by his parents from the moment of conception, he won a favoured place in his community through the development of his practical, social and intellectual skills. Certainly by the time we hear of him at the marriage feast in Cana it is clear that he is socially assured and utterly at ease with his own authority. It seems, too, that he has a sense of fun as well as a natural sympathy for the predicament of others. The person who is about to embark on the life of the radical and charismatic outsider is literally the life and soul of the party.

It is also evident that Jesus was a highly articulate man. Not only is he steeped in the Jewish scriptures but he is capable of employing language to tell stories which draw their raw material from the world around him while infusing it with symbolic meaning of the profoundest intensity. In this sense Jesus is a poetic orator, capable of using language at its most richly expressive. But it is not only with groups and crowds that he shows himself to be so verbally accomplished. It is also clear that he is at home with the language of intimacy for otherwise it is difficult to understand how he could have won such devoted affection from his followers and especially from the women among them. When after the resurrection we witness his meeting in the garden with the sorrowing Mary Magdalen we are in the presence of a man who can convey the deepest love simply by uttering the name of the beloved. The fact, too, that on this occasion he restrains Mary from physical embrace suggests that she had come to know him as a person whose physical responsiveness was as sensitive and spontaneous as his use of language. Language itself is stretched to breaking point when we ponder the amazing significance of Jesus as the incarnate Lord.

Perhaps the most daunting idea for anyone attempting to live out a Christian life is the suggestion that we are called to 'imitate' Christ. In some ways this notion is preposterous for clearly the society and culture of Jesus's time were utterly different to our own and to 'imitate' him might be to court a bizarre and anachronistic way of being which would render us eccentric in the extreme and alienate most of our contemporaries. At a deeper level, however, we are invited in faith to explore the furthest limits of our human potential and to discover what it might mean, like Jesus, to become fully human. In this sense, our goal is to celebrate our own identity with as clear an affirmation of unique personhood as that uttered by Jesus in his authoritative 'I am'. Such a celebration is the outcome not of self-centredness and self-absorption but of self-love which comes from acknowledging that in our innermost being we are acceptable and desirable to the God who sustains us.

As I pondered on the personality of Jesus and on what imitation might mean, I was suddenly and startlingly aware that I have chosen a profession where I catch unmistakeable glimpses of my Lord every day of my working life. Recently, for example, I was awestruck as I read the account of the relationship one of my trainees is currently forging with a woman who experienced sexual abuse from

her father and her brother throughout most of her adolescence. My awe springs from the realisation of the healing
that is being wrought in and through this relationship and
by the attributes that are revealed unobtrusively and
almost as a matter of course in both the client and in the
trainee therapist who is seeking to be with her in her pain.

Like this sexually-abused woman, many clients who
arrive at the therapist's door have certainly never been
welcomed into life. On the contrary they have often been
rejected, ignored or unwanted. Gradually, however, as they
begin to experience and to trust the therapist's acceptance
and the validation which springs from the therapist's
understanding and cherishing of them, so they begin to feel
at home in the created world. Resentment and bitterness
can be fully experienced and then exorcised so that they
can begin to take their place in a society which previously
they had both hated and feared. Such a reconciliation
is often the prelude to the first glimmerings of personal
uniqueness and the possibility of new meaning. In brief,
acceptance by another leads to a sense of belonging to
the wider society which in turn engenders a level of self-
acceptance from which the experience of personal uniqueness can spring.

My sense of being in a privileged profession is even
further heightened when I consider how in therapy tongues
are unloosed and language takes on a new and often mysterious beauty. Not only, it seems, do I glimpse my Lord
but I also hear his voice. It is my experience that at the
beginning of therapy a client is commonly unambitious in
the use of language. Even when great distress pushes him
or her into verbal expression which seems unstoppable,
there is usually a pedestrian and repetitive quality about
the language employed. As therapy proceeds, however, and
the client risks confronting feelings in the present moment
there is often a perceptible shift in the use of words. Images
and metaphors begin to abound and the client is concerned
to seek the 'mot juste' and to discover the adjective which

most nearly describes the subtle nuance of meaning he or she wishes to convey or the elusive feeling which suddenly and unpredictably rises up from memories long since buried in the unconscious. Indeed there is a whole discipline of counselling called 'focusing' which encourages clients to track down a 'felt sense' and to find appropriate language to describe their discovery. It is not, I believe, unduly fanciful to suggest that when therapy is proceeding well the client gradually begins to extend the boundaries of his or her use of language and to discover an articulacy which had previously lain dormant or unexploited. One client once remarked to me that he had had no idea that he could talk 'like a poet' until he entered therapy and others have been genuinely startled by the images and metaphors which cross their lips in the course of a counselling session. It is as if language ceases to be a smoke-screen for concealing the inner world of the person: instead it is transparent in the sense that it becomes the means through which the person is revealed to the world in all his or her complexity. Language is the sacred medium for the expression of wholeness.

For many clients in therapy it is not only language but also the body which is released into new life. The physical responsiveness of Jesus to those about him is seldom mirrored in the life of the conventional Christian congregation but for many Christians the sacrament of the Eucharist does at least provide a reminder that their faith is as much about the body as the soul. At the moment of communion they touch their Lord and are united to him as if in a physical embrace. The joy of being physically enfolded is too deep for words but where it is absent the pain, too, can be inexpressible. Such an absence commonly characterises many of those who find themselves in therapy and as I reflect on this I wonder whose presence is at work in the transformation of the body which I am so often moved to witness during the therapeutic process. It is not uncommon for the person who is struggling with deep and long-standing distress to feel alienated from his or her body and to respond stiffly and awkwardly to the overtures of others. Tightly crossed arms, clenched jaws and crossed legs are not infrequently the outward signs of the frightened and distrustful person. He or she cannot comfortably be at home in the body and has often found it necessary to cut off from physical (and sexual) sensations altogether. It is as if the experience of being 'incarnate' is too painful to be endured. As therapy proceeds, however, such persons begin cautiously to relax and to let go. Some even experience an exquisitely painful tingling in their limbs as they allow life to flow into them. For me there often comes the precious moment when I know that it is appropriate to touch a client for the first time because now he or she is 'embodied' and no longer afraid. At that moment we enter into a deeper communion for we are 'in touch' as incarnate beings and can no longer deny our capacity to confer blessing on each other.

I am aware of the enormity of what I am saying in these reflections on the process of therapy. I am making the claim that therapeutic relationships, when they go well, have the potential for enabling persons to become more 'Christ-like', to reveal more clearly their divine attributes. That is to say such relationships make it possible for human beings to feel welcomed into the world, to sense their uniqueness and their purpose, to discover the sacredness and the wonder of language and to celebrate their physical natures. I do not wish to retract these reflections because I believe them to be true. At the same time, however, I am acutely aware that therapy seldom leads people into calm waters or emotional serenity. Instead it seems frequently to bring about a suffering of a wholly different order to the pain and distress which may well have brought the client to therapy in the first place.

This new order of suffering is undoubtedly brought about through the operation of empathy. To be understood with love is the prelude to understanding with love. Empathy brings with it an expansion of consciousness which makes it increasingly impossible to be blind to the pain of others and to the anguish of the world. Not that others (or the world for that matter) necessarily welcome such an extension of consciousness. To be understood can be intolerable for it may bring with it the confrontation with annihilating guilt or the recognition of an inner life invaded and dominated by the forces of darkness. In the course of therapy therefore as a client is enabled to take the risk of extending loving understanding to himself and to others, so he learns what it means both to bear the pain of another's suffering and to experience utter rejection at the hands of those who in Blake's words cannot 'bear the beams of love'.

It is as I reflect on the Passion of Jesus, however, that the well-nigh inevitability of such a process becomes clear. Jesus, as we have seen, was as secure in his identity as any human being has ever been. He was welcomed into the world, loved devotedly, respected by his elders and fully-integrated into the society and culture of his day. It was precisely this wholeness of being, however, that led him inexorably into suffering and death for it made him, in the words of the German poet, Rainer Maria Rilke, no longer at home in the interpreted world. As he came more and more to live out his vision and to follow the vocation demanded by his Father's business, so the world in which he found himself was increasingly unable to support his presence. The full humanness of Jesus in all its glory was finally an intolerable affront to those weighed down with guilt, anxiety, ambition, fear and the lust for power. What is more the humanity of Jesus, which in its completeness revealed his divinity was at the same time the manifestation of utter vulnerability. The life of Jesus Christ, the incarnate God, reveals that to be fully human means to embody a vulnerability which may well court and invite a wounding unto death.

Jesus was both a great lover and greatly loved. It is my experience that those who have found healing through a relationship with a therapist always discover that they, too, are lovable and capable of loving. They are able, often for the first time, to glimpse what it might mean to be fully human but with this discovery comes the vulnerability which inevitably accompanies the one who dares to love and be loved. It is for this reason that I now warn clients that they are embarking on a dangerous enterprise. Should it bring about not merely an alleviation of problems but a healing of their fragmented humanity then they, too, will no longer be at home in the interpreted world and will suffer the agony of their yearning for another home. To those who are bold or foolish enough to contemplate training as therapists I can only whisper words of love and caution for their task is too awesome to bear overmuch scrutiny. It may seem a far cry from the counsellor's consulting room to the cross of dereliction. I am persuaded, however, that the distance between these may suddenly and unexpectedly narrow. Every time I sit down with my client I know that we risk glimpsing God in each other and that if this should occur we may be swept along our own via dolorosa. It is not always easy at such times to remember that Jesus made the 'one full, perfect and sufficient sacrifice, oblation and satisfaction for the sins of the whole world' and that we are called to be Easter people. Hope lies beyond despair and 'all shall be well'. In the familiar words of Mother Julian of Norwich we hear the confident assertion of one who prayed that she might be privileged to share in the suffering and death of her Lord and whose prayer was granted. It is her testimony which upholds me as I dare to enter into the mind of Jesus and it is her faith which sustains me as each day I utter those seemingly simple words, 'How can I be of help to you?'

Questions for Reflection

1. What kind of welcome into the world do you believe you received as a baby? If you have children what kind of welcome did you give them?
2. At the age of twelve Jesus was already following his vocation. In our own culture how respectful are we of children and adolescents and how do we encourage their sense of purpose?
3. Do you treat language as the sacred medium for the expression of wholeness or are you content to speak soullessly and without care?
4. Are you able to cherish your body and celebrate its wonder or are you ashamed of it and prone to do it harm?
5. Do you try to listen to others and to understand their inner worlds and if you do how do you bear the pain which you find there?

Appendix 1

The Passion according to St John[1]

It was before the Passover festival. Jesus knew that his hour had come and he must leave this world and go to the Father. He had always loved his own who were in the world, and now he was to show the full extent of his love.

The devil had already put it into the mind of Judas son of Simon Iscariot to betray him. During supper, Jesus, well aware that the Father had entrusted everything to him, and that he had come from God and was going back to God, rose from table, laid aside his garments, and taking a towel, tied it round him. Then he poured water into a basin, and began to wash his disciples' feet and to wipe them with the towel.

When it was Simon Peter's turn, Peter said to him, 'You, Lord, washing my feet?' Jesus replied, 'You do not understand now what I am doing, but one day you will.' Peter said, 'I will never let you wash my feet.' 'If I do not wash you,' Jesus replied, 'you are not in fellowship with me.' 'Then, Lord,' said Simon Peter, 'not my feet only; wash my hands and head as well!'

Jesus said, 'A man who has bathed needs no further washing; he is altogether clean; and you are clean, though not every one of you.' He added the words 'not every one of you' because he knew who was going to betray him.

After washing their feet and taking his garments again, he sat down. 'Do you understand what I have done for

---

[1] Taken from the *New English Bible*, second edition © 1970 by permission of Oxford and Cambridge University Presses.

you?' he asked. 'You call me "Master" and "Lord", and rightly so, for that is what I am. Then if I, your Lord and Master, have washed your feet, you also ought to wash one another's feet. I have set you an example: you are to do as I have done for you. In very truth I tell you, a servant is not greater than his master, nor a messenger than the one who sent him. If you know this, happy are you if you act upon it.

'I am not speaking about all of you; I know whom I have chosen. But there is a text of Scripture to be fulfilled: "He who eats bread with me has turned against me." I tell you this now, before the event, so that when it happens you may believe that I am what I am. In very truth I tell you, he who receives any messenger of mine receives me; receiving me, he receives the One who sent me.'

After saying this, Jesus exclaimed in deep agitation of spirit, 'In truth in very truth I tell you, one of you is going to betray me.' The disciples looked at one another in bewilderment: whom could he be speaking of? One of them, the disciple he loved, was reclining close beside Jesus. So Simon Peter nodded to him and said, 'Ask who it is he means.' That disciple, as he reclined, leaned back close to Jesus and asked, 'Lord, who is it?' Jesus replied, 'It is the man to whom I give this piece of bread when I have dipped it in the dish.' Then, after dipping it in the dish, he took it out and gave it to Judas son of Simon Iscariot. As soon as Judas had received it Satan entered him. Jesus said to him, 'Do quickly what you have to do.' No one at the table understood what he meant by this. Some supposed that, as Judas was in charge of the common purse, Jesus was telling him to buy what was needed for the festival, or to make some gift to the poor. As soon as Judas had received the bread he went out. It was night.

(13:1–30)

After these words, Jesus went out with his disciples, and crossed the Kedron ravine. There was a garden there, and

he and his disciples went into it. The place was known to
Judas, his betrayer, because Jesus had often met there with
his disciples. So Judas took a detachment of soldiers, and
police provided by the chief priests and the Pharisees,
equipped with lanterns, torches, and weapons, and made
his way to the garden. Jesus, knowing all that was coming
upon him, went out to them and asked, 'Who is it you
want?' 'Jesus of Nazareth', they answered. Jesus said, 'I
am he.' And there stood Judas the traitor with them. When
he said, 'I am he', they drew back and fell to the ground.
Again Jesus asked, 'Who is it you want?' 'Jesus of Nazareth', they answered. Then Jesus said, 'I have told you that
I am he. If I am the man you want, let these others go.'
(This was to make good his words, 'I have not lost one of
those whom thou gavest me.') Thereupon Simon Peter
drew the sword he was wearing and struck at the High
Priest's servant, cutting off his right ear. (The servant's
name was Malchus.) Jesus said to Peter, 'Sheathe your
sword. This is the cup the Father has given me; shall I not
drink it?'

The troops with their commander, and the Jewish police,
now arrested Jesus and secured him. They took him first
to Annas. Annas was father-in-law of Caiaphas, the High
Priest for that year – the same Caiaphas who had advised
the Jews that it would be to their interest if one man died
for the whole people. Jesus was followed by Simon Peter
and another disciple. This disciple, who was acquainted
with the High Priest, went with Jesus into the High Priest's
courtyard, but Peter halted at the door outside. So the
other disciple, the High Priest's acquaintance, went out
again and spoke to the woman at the door, and brought
Peter in. The maid on duty at the door said to Peter, 'Are
you another of this man's disciples?' 'I am not', he said.
The servants and the police had made a charcoal fire,
because it was cold, and were standing round it warming
themselves. And Peter too was standing with them, sharing
the warmth.

The High Priest questioned Jesus about his disciples and about what he taught. Jesus replied, 'I have spoken openly to all the world; I have always taught in synagogue and in the temple, where all Jews congregate; I have said nothing in secret. Why question me? Ask my hearers what I told them; they know what I said.' When he said this, one of the police who was standing next to him struck him on the face, exclaiming, 'Is that the way to answer the High Priest?' Jesus replied, 'If I spoke amiss, state it in evidence; if I spoke well, why strike me?'

So Annas sent him bound to Caiaphas the High Priest.

Meanwhile Simon Peter stood warming himself. The others asked, 'Are you another of his disciples?' But he denied it: 'I am not', he said. One of the High Priest's servants, a relation of the man whose ear Peter had cut off, insisted, 'Did I not see you with him in the garden?' Peter denied again; and just then a cock crew.

From Caiaphas Jesus was led into the Governor's head-quarters. It was now early morning, and the Jews themselves stayed outside the headquarters to avoid defilement, so that they could eat the Passover meal. So Pilate went out to them and asked, 'What charge do you bring against this man?' 'If he were not a criminal,' they replied, 'we should not have brought him before you.' Pilate said, 'Take him away and try him by your own law.' The Jews answered, 'We are not allowed to put any man to death.' Thus they ensured the fulfilment of the words by which Jesus had indicated the manner of his death.

Pilate then went back into his headquarters and summoned Jesus. 'Are you the king of the Jews?' he asked. Jesus said, 'Is that your own idea, or have others suggested it to you?' 'What! am I a Jew?' said Pilate. 'Your own nation and their chief priests have brought you before me. What have you done?' Jesus replied, 'My kingdom does not belong to this world. If it did, my followers would be fighting to save me from arrest by the Jews. My kingly authority comes from elsewhere.' 'You are a king, then?'

said Pilate. Jesus answered, ' "King" is your word. My task is to bear witness to the truth. For this was I born; for this I came into the world, and all who are not deaf to truth listen to my voice.' Pilate said, 'What is truth?', and with those words went out again to the Jews. 'For my part,' he said, 'I find no case against him. But you have a custom that I release one prisoner for you at Passover. Would you like me to release the king of the Jews?' Again the clamour rose: 'Not him; we want Barabbas!' (Barabbas was a bandit.)

(18)

Pilate now took Jesus and had him flogged; and the soldiers plaited a crown of thorns and placed it on his head, and robed him in a purple cloak. Then time after time they came up to him, crying, 'Hail, King of the Jews!', and struck him on the face.

Once more Pilate came out and said to the Jews, 'Here he is; I am bringing him out to let you know that I find no case against him'; and Jesus came out, wearing the crown of thorns and the purple cloak. 'Behold the Man!' said Pilate. The chief priests and their henchmen saw him and shouted, 'Crucify! crucify!' 'Take him and crucify him yourselves,' said Pilate; 'for my part I find no case against him.' The Jews answered, 'We have a law; and by that law he ought to die, because he has claimed to be Son of God.'

When Pilate heard that, he was more afraid than ever, and going back into his headquarters he asked Jesus, 'Where have you come from?' But Jesus gave him no answer. 'Do you refuse to speak to me?' said Pilate. 'Surely you know that I have authority to release you, and I have authority to crucify you?' 'You would have no authority at all over me', Jesus replied, 'if it had not been granted you from above; and therefore the deeper guilt lies with the man who handed me over to you.'

From that moment Pilate tried hard to release him; but

APPENDIX 1

the Jews kept shouting, 'If you let this man go, you are no friend to Caesar; any man who claims to be a king is defying Caesar.' When Pilate heard what they were saying, he brought Jesus out and took his seat on the tribunal at the place known as 'The Pavement' ('Gabbatha' in the language of the Jews). It was the eve of Passover, about noon. Pilate said to the Jews, 'Here is your king.' They shouted, 'Away with him! Away with him! Crucify him!' 'Crucify your king?' said Pilate. 'We have no king but Caesar', the Jews replied. Then at last, to satisfy them, he handed Jesus over to be crucified.

Jesus was now taken in charge and, carrying his own cross, went out to the Place of the Skull, as it is called (or, in the Jews' language, 'Golgotha'), where they crucified him, and with him two others, one on the right, one on the left, and Jesus between them.

And Pilate wrote an inscription to be fastened to the cross; it read, 'Jesus of Nazareth King of the Jews.' This inscription was read by many Jews, because the place where Jesus was crucified was not far from the city, and the inscription was in Hebrew, Latin, and Greek. Then the Jewish chief priests said to Pilate, 'You should not write "King of the Jews"; write, "He claimed to be king of the Jews."' Pilate replied, 'What I have written, I have written.'

The soldiers, having crucified Jesus, took possession of his clothes, and divided them into four parts, one for each soldier, leaving out the tunic. The tunic was seamless, woven in one piece throughout; so they said to one another, 'We must not tear this; let us toss for it'; and thus the text of Scripture came true: 'They shared my garments among them, and cast lots for my clothing.'

That is what the soldiers did. But meanwhile near the cross where Jesus hung stood his mother, with her sister, Mary wife of Clopas, and Mary of Magdala. Jesus saw his mother, with the disciple whom he loved standing beside her. He said to her, 'Mother, there is your son'; and to the disciple, 'There is your mother'; and from that moment the disciple took her into his home.

After that, Jesus, aware that all had now come to its appointed end, said in fulfilment of Scripture, 'I thirst.' A jar stood there full of sour wine; so they soaked a sponge with the wine, fixed it on a javelin, and held it up to his lips. Having received the wine, he said, 'It is accomplished!' He bowed his head and gave up his spirit.

(19:1–30)

Appendix 2

Guide to Personal Meditation

For Catholic readers and many from other traditions, too, the Stations of the Cross and the Sorrowful Mysteries of the Rosary will have deepened and enriched their understanding of the Passion perhaps over many years. Such 'classical' aids to reflection are beyond price and offer the individual the freedom to explore unknown terrain within the supportive framework of a familiar structure. There are also many well-known and well-loved prayers and hymns which can penetrate deep into the mystery of suffering and redemption.

It is not my intention in this brief appendix to explore such well-tried resources. Instead I have assembled here a number of less familiar extracts, together with passages from this book, which I believe can lead to a deeper empathic understanding of Jesus and those who were around him in the final days of his earthly life. As a therapist I treasure this capacity to empathise perhaps more than any other single ability. If I can somehow enter another's world and experience reality as he or she experiences it without, however, losing touch with my own, then there is a good chance that I shall be able to love with understanding. Empathy for me is, in short, the royal road to loving and being loved. It was this kind of love that I experienced as a nine year old child and in a sense this whole book is an attempt to reciprocate the gift that transformed my existence at that time. God calls us to be not servants but friends and such a calling requires of us a preparedness to establish a relationship of mutuality. It is

difficult to believe that God desires our love and understanding let alone that he needs it. Perhaps it is our reluc-
tance to face this amazing possibility which keeps us locked
in passive dependency or guilty revolt. Certainly a mutual
relationship calls for an exercising of the will and the
imagination which cannot be lightly undertaken. Few
people even manage it with their families and spouses, for
empathy, I would suggest, is rarely the leading character-
istic of family or marital life. My hope is that as we attempt
to enter more deeply into the mind and heart of Jesus and
into the inner worlds of those who took part in the events
leading up to his death so we shall come to recognise our
common kinship and the reality of our membership one of
another.

The process for reflection and meditation which I suggest
is as follows:

1. Read the extract several times and, if you have a reten-
tive memory, learn it by heart.
2. Try to put yourself in the shoes of the person who figures
centrally in the extract and ask yourself: 'What is it like
to be this person?'
3. Try to be in touch with the feelings and thoughts gener-
ated *in you* by the person with whom you have attempted
to empathise. Ask yourself 'How does it feel to be with
this person?'
4. Imagine that you are entering into dialogue with the
person or persons concerned. What do you find yourself
saying?
5. Stay silent in the presence of the other for a short while
and then conclude with the words of Julian of Norwich:
'All shall be well, and all shall be well, and all manner
of thing shall be well'. Amen.

The whole process needs 15 to 30 minutes. Clearly the
extracts used here are merely illustrations and in no way

exhaustive. Readers will know and discover many others which serve equally well, if not better, to lead them into the heart of God and into the sanctuary of their own hearts where God is already waiting.

1. *Jesus*
   I am a man, yet I am the Son of God: so are you. All you have to do is realise it. (Sydney Carter, *Dance in the Dark*, London, Collins Fount, 1980)

2. *Jesus*
   'Is not this the carpenter's son?' (Matthew 13:55)

3. *Mary Magdalen*
   Love has to be expressed. You cannot dam it up by conventions and rules. I don't care what insinuations people chose to make. (Margaret Magdalen csmv, *Transformed by Love*, London, Darton, Longman and Todd, 1989)

4. *Mary, the mother of Jesus*
   She claims no crown from Christ apart,
   Who gave God life and limb,
   She only claims a broken heart
   Because of Him.

   (C. A. Studdert Kennedy,
   'Good Friday falls on Lady Day'
   in *The Unutterable Beauty*, London, Mowbray, 1983)

5. *Judas*
   'Twas the Bridegroom stood at the open door,
      And beckon'd, smiling sweet;
   'Twas the soul of Judas Iscariot
      Stole in, and fell at his feet

The supper wine is pour'd at last,
  The lights burn bright and fair,
Iscariot washes the Bridegroom's feet,
  And dries them with his hair.
                    (Robert Williams Buchanan, 'Judas Iscariot'
                              quoted in Charles Causley ed.,
                    The Sun Dancing, London, Penguin, 1982)

6. *Pilate, Caiaphas and the rest*
   They were the real prisoners – Pilate, Caiaphas and the
   rest. They were the real corpses in the tomb. (Stephen
   Verney, *The Dance of Love*, London, Collins Fount, 1989)

7. *The Penitent Thief*
   It was in the racket of a crowd of sadists revelling in
       pain
   And their screeches, howls, curses and shouts
   That you heard the profound cry of the breaking heart
       of their prey:
   'Why hast thou forsaken me?'
                          (Saunders Lewis, 'To the Good Thief',
                          trans. Gwyn Thomas, in Alun R. Jones and
                          Gwyn Thomas eds, *Presenting Saunders Lewis*,
                          University of Wales Press, 1973)

8. *Jesus*
   He is consumed with a sense of the powerlessness of his
   own love to keep Judas in relationship with him. (see
   above pp. 13–14)

9. *Jesus*
   He is self-possessed, full of light and compassion and
   yet faced with the implacable force of religious fear and
   hatred he is powerless to resist. (p. 19)

10. *Jesus*

In his last hours Jesus is loved and supported by women whose love is faithful and fearless to the end. Jesus on the cross experiences the love of women as capable of taking on the cosmic forces of darkness. (pp. 40–1)

11. *John*

He only a few hours previously has been powerless to stretch out to the treacherous Judas, but now he is at the foot of the cross, the only man who dares to give expression to his love and tenderness. (p. 45)

12. *Jesus*

Jesus leaves the Upper Room and goes out into the night, his heart breaking for Judas and weighed down with sorrow at the apparent indifference of the others to Judas's plight. (p. 14)

13. *Jesus*

As Jesus stands before Annas and then before Caiaphas he suffers the depth of anguish which comes from being truly himself only to discover that in doing so he is despised, condemned and rejected by those who profess to serve the same God that resides in his own heart. (p. 22)

14. *Pilate*

Pilate wriggles and squirms in order not to become Jesus's executioner. (p. 26)

15. *Pilate*

Pilate is forced by his role into complete inauthenticity. (p. 27)

16. *Pilate*

His racial prejudice is such that he cannot engage with Jesus in rational discourse. (p. 27)

17. *Jesus*

This naked and utterly defenceless man cries out in agony not only because of intolerable physical pain but out of love for all those whose lives are in thrall to any authority which is blind to the wonder and fragility of human nature. (p. 33)

18. *Jesus*

For Jesus there is the overwhelming proximity of the soldiers whose bodies were presumably young, athletic and full of animal vigour. (pp. 33–4)

19. *Jesus*

. . . you must have loved Mary Magdalene
who was beautiful
and smelled of flowers.

> (Ernst Eggimann, *Jesustexte*, Zurich, 1972,
> quoted above p.36)

20. *Jesus*

As we remember his moving and intimate conversations with his mother, with Mary and Martha from Bethany, with the Samaritan woman at the well . . . with the woman caught in adultery, it comes as no surprise to learn that Jesus was much loved by women. (pp. 39–40)

21. *Jesus*

He knows what it means to feel utterly desperate, abandoned by the God in whom he had placed his complete trust. (p. 44)

22. *Jesus*

We want to distance ourselves from the dying Christ as if he is not really one of us at all. But he is *and* he is the Son of God. (p. 46)